motorsports

MOTORCYCLES

Paul Mason

amicus
mankato, minnesota

Published by Amicus
P.O. Box 1329, Mankato, Minnesota 56002

Printed in the United States of America by
Bang Printing, Brainerd, Minnesota.

Published by arrangement with the Watts
Publishing Group Ltd., London.

Library of Congress Cataloging-in-Publication Data
Mason, Paul, 1967-
  Motorcycles / by Paul Mason.
    p. cm. -- (Motorsports)
  Includes index.
  Summary: "Explains the history of motorcycle
racing and the how-to of the sport"--Provided by
publisher.
  ISBN 978-1-60753-121-0 (library binding)
  1. Motorcycle racing--Juvenile literature. 2.
Motorcycles, Racing--Juvenile literature. I. Title.
  GV1060.M35 2011
  796.7--dc22
                                    2009034371

Planning and production by
Tall Tree Limited
Editor: Rob Colson
Designer: Jonathan Vipond

Picture credits:
Apollo Motors: 23
Corbis: 11 bottom (Jean-Yves Ruszniewski/
TempSport), 29 middle left (Nic Bothma/epa).
Dreamstime: cover middle (Shaiful Rizal Mohd
Jaafar), cover bottom left (Sergey Goruppa), cover
bottom middle (Ahmad Faizal Yahya), cover
bottom right (Paul Brennan), 3 (EchoArt),
6 (Shaiful Rizal Mohd Jaafar), 7 (Shariffc), 9
bottom (Amaviael), 10–11 (Afby71), 12–13
(Afby71), 20 (Imagestalk), 22 (Moori), 24
(Tomashko), 25 (Sportlibrary), 29 bottom left
(Warren Price), 29 middle right (Baumstamm),
29 bottom right (Afby71).
Getty: 8 (Ian Walton), 9 top (Popperfoto), 14–15, 15
top right (AFP), 16, 17, 18–19, 21 (AFP), 26, 27
(AFP), 29 top left, 29 top right (AFP).
IStockphoto: 12 bottom left (Richard Laurence), 13
bottom right (jallfree), 19 bottom right
(gianlucabartoli).

1208
32010

9 8 7 6 5 4 3 2 1

CONTENTS

MOTORCYCLE RACING

Nothing smells and sounds like the start of a motorcycle race. The smell of oil and exhaust fumes is unmistakable. Spectators cover their ears at the wail of the exhausts as the racers dump the clutch and speed away from the start line.

THE WORLD OF BIKE RACING

Road, racetrack, or dirt trail—if you can ride a motorcycle on it, you can have a race. Racers usually specialize in either track racing or off-road racing.

▷ Don't try this at home! Japanese rider Shinya Nakano does a massive wheelie at the end of a race.

WINNING A CHAMPIONSHIP

Most championships are decided after a series of races. Together these are called a **season**. Riders are awarded points in each race, depending on where they finish. At the end of the season, the rider with the most points is the champion.

△ Children as young as eight compete in motocross races such as this one in Sepang, Malaysia.

RACE TEAMS

Top riders are always part of a team. In big championships, most teams have two riders. The team whose riders get the most points wins a second championship. This is called a **constructors' championship**.

TECHNICAL DATA

The longest jump ever landed on a dirt bike is 321.5 feet (98 m), by Australia's Robbie Maddison in 2007.

EARLY DAYS OF RACING

The first motorcycle racers were very brave. They raced rattling machines on ordinary roads that had been closed to traffic. A mistake meant crashing into a wall or a tree and would almost certainly be fatal.

THE TOURIST TROPHY

The first big international motorcycle race was the Isle of Man Tourist Trophy. Bikers around the world call this the TT. The first TT was held in 1907. The race is still held every year, despite campaigns to stop it because it is so dangerous.

▽ *British rider John McGuinness takes off over a bump on his way to victory at the 2007 TT.*

ROAD RACING GROWS

As motorcycles became more popular during the twentieth century, so did racing them. Soon, races were being held across the world. Many different kinds of races were held, such as races on boards built for bicycles or with a sidecar attached.

▷ *A sidecar race at Crystal Palace, London, in 1928. The rider and passenger work together to maintain balance.*

DIRT-TRACK RACING

In the United States, racing on oval racetracks was more popular than racing on the roads. The oval tracks often had dirt or **cinder** surfaces, so the racers slid around spectacularly. Today, crowds of U.S. motorcycle-racing fans still flock to dirt-track racing. In Europe, speedway riding is a popular form of dirt-track racing. In cold northern European countries, specially adapted bikes even race around on snowy courses.

▽ *Dirt-track machines have no gears or brakes. They turn by sliding sideways.*

TRACK RACING

After World War II (1939–1945), more motorcycle races were held on specially built racetracks. The new tracks were safer for the riders and fans. The fans could sit and watch the action better from specially built viewing points or grandstands.

RACING CATEGORIES

Today, track racing is divided up into different categories. The top class of racing is MotoGP. MotoGP bikes each cost hundreds of thousands of dollars to make. Teams with less money take part in Superbike racing. Superbikes are based on **production motorcycles**, which anybody can buy.

△ *250cc bikes race at Sepang, Malaysia. The 125cc and 250cc races are held before the main event, the MotoGP.*

FACTORY TEAMS

Every racer dreams of riding for a factory team. Factory-team riders get the best motorcycles because they are supported by motorcycle manufacturers. The manufacturers hope that if other riders see their bikes winning races, the riders will decide to buy one.

TECHNICAL DATA

These are the main track racing classes:

- MotoGP
- 600cc
- 125cc
- Superbikes
- Supersport

THE RIDERS

At first, most motorcycle racers came from the U.S. or Europe. Today, however, racing is popular all around the world. The top riders come from Europe, North and South America, Japan, and Australia.

◁ Italian Giacomo Agostini was probably the greatest motorcycle racer ever. Between 1966 and 1975, he won 122 grand prix.

MotoGP MACHINES

MotoGP is the highest class of motorcycle racing. The world's best riders battle it out on lightning-fast machines, sometimes rubbing shoulders through the turns at over 100 mph (160 km/h). They ride the most advanced bikes in the world.

TIRES

Choosing the right tire can be the difference between winning and losing. There are special tires for wet or dry weather conditions. Tires must be hot to grip the road properly, so they are kept in tire warmers (see below) before the race.

THE BIKE

MotoGP bikes produce about 240 **bhp**— twice as much power as most family cars but with less than an eighth of the weight! They can leap from standing still to 62 mph (100 km/h) in just a couple of seconds.

BRAKES

Motorbikes slow down when the brake pads grip discs attached to the wheels. There are two discs on the front wheel and one on the rear. The front brake does most of the slowing-down work. Sometimes, a rider brakes so hard that the rear wheel lifts up. This is known as doing an "**endo**."

Brake disc

▲ *Italian Valentino Rossi riding for the Fiat Yamaha team.*

THE RIDER'S TEAM

Even the greatest riders don't win races on their own. A team of experts supports them. They, too, share the glory and often win **bonuses** if one of the riders performs well.

PIT CREW

In top race teams, riders have a large team of people helping them. Data analysts look at records of how the motorcycle works and suggest changes and improvements. Mechanics fine-tune the engine, change wheels and tires, and rebuild the motorcycles after a crash.

▷ Inside the MotoGP garage of the Ducati team during testing at Jerez in Spain.

BIKE DESIGN

In MotoGP, factory teams have a newly designed bike every year. Work on the design starts months before the racing season. Other teams—called **satellite teams**— get to use similar motorcycles. They never get the latest versions, though, in case they beat the factory team!

△ *The Kawasaki factory team races the latest MotoGP version of its Ninja motorcycle series.*

TECHNICAL DATA

In 2008, Casey Stoner set a MotoGP speed record when his Ducati reached 213.2 mph (343.2 km/h). (For comparison, the fastest modern Formula 1 car traveled 229.8 mph (369.9 km/h) in 2004.)

PIT BOSS

Once a new motorcycle has been developed, the suspension, tires, and engine can all be changed to suit the rider. The team's **pit boss** works closely with the rider to make sure the motorcycle rides exactly how he or she wants it.

MotoGP RACE WEEKEND

A MotoGP rider who wants to stand on the winner's **podium** first has to get through practice and qualifying. Qualifying is very important. If riders fail to perform well in the qualifying session, they have almost no chance of winning the actual race.

In Saturday's qualifying sessions, the riders aim to record the fastest lap. By now they should have the suspension, tire, and engine settings right—but they may still be making changes to squeeze some extra speed from their motorcycles!

1. PRACTICE

Practice usually begins on Friday. The riders use the practice session to get used to the twists and turns of the track. They test the tires and suspension to get the best settings for the motorcycle and track. They also find out where all the bumps are!

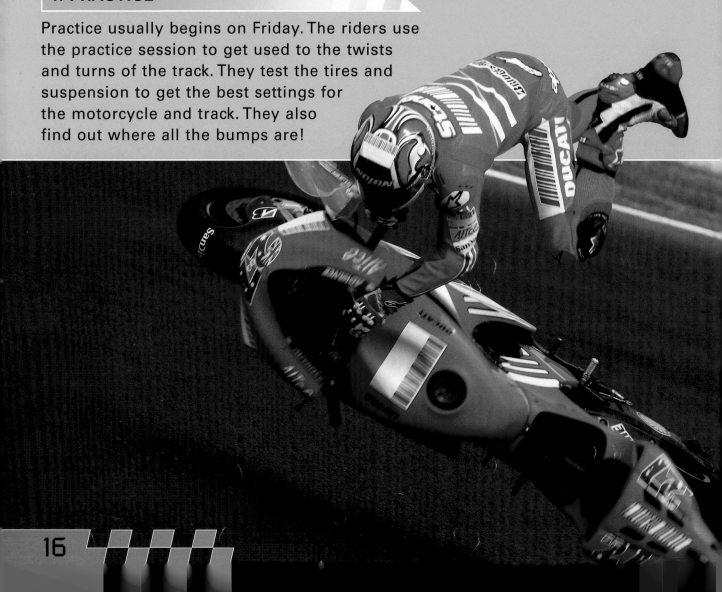

THE STARTING GRID

Whoever is fastest at the end of qualifying starts the race at the front of Sunday's **starting grid**. This is known as the **pole position**. It's a big advantage to be near the front—most race winners start from the front three rows of the grid.

◁ Casey Stoner loses control of several hundred thousand dollars' worth of MotoGP bike and crashes during practice for the Australian MotoGP in 2007.

△ The front of the starting grid at the Australian MotoGP.

TECHNICAL DATA

In 2008 at the U.S. MotoGP race, Valentino Rossi became the most successful top-class rider ever. He set a new world record by winning his 69th top-class race.

RACE DAY

Race weekends feature more than one class of racing. In the lower divisions, with smaller-engined bikes such as the 125cc racers, the racing is often close and exciting. It gets the spectators warmed up for the main event—the MotoGP.

▽ *The leading racers all aim to get the "hole shot"—to reach the first corner first. If you can manage that, other people will have to overtake you to win!*

FORMING THE GRID

As the start time draws near, the riders line up on the grid. At first, this is a bit **chaotic**. There are engineers, and "umbrella girls" holding umbrellas to shade the riders. You might even bump into a celebrity wandering around.

SIGHTING LAP

A few minutes before the start, the grid clears. The riders start off on a "sighting lap," warming up their bike engines, tires, and brakes. When they get back to the grid and into position, one red signal light after another goes on until all five are lit. When the lights go out, it's GO! The racers speed away from the line.

TECHNICAL DATA

The youngest ever top-class MotoGP winner was American Freddie Spencer. He was just 20 years and 196 days old when he won the Belgian MotoGP in 1982.

RACE TACTICS

Motorcycle racers can't go full speed all the way to the finish. If they go as fast as they can at the beginning, their tires wear out. So they have to decide the best tactics—which part of the race to go fastest in, and when to ease off.

▷ *By the end of a race, the tires of a MotoGP motorcycle are dirty and worn.*

OFF-ROAD RACING

Some off-road bike racers enjoy racing for days across a desert. Others spend their time speeding around the jumps and bumps in short races around motocross circuits. Whatever kind of thrill you're after, off-road racing has something for everyone.

MOTOCROSS AND SUPERCROSS

Motocross (MX) and supercross (SX) races are short, often lasting just a few minutes. The riders use light, zippy bikes with **long-travel suspension**. The courses feature jumps, bumps, and tight turns. This type of racing demands high levels of fitness and excellent bike-handling skills. MX races are held on natural circuits and are always outdoors. SX races happen on circuits made of tons of dirt piled up by bulldozers. SX races may be held in sports stadiums, sometimes even indoors!

▷ Riders fly into the air at the top of a bump during a supermotard race (a type of motocross), in which riders race on a course that is part road, part dirt track.

ENDURO RACING

Enduro races can last anything from a few hours to over a week. "Enduro" stands for endurance— and however long they last, the races are always tough. The riders have to find their own way and even repair their own bikes if there's a problem.

▽ *Italian rider Fabrizio Meoni rides through the Mauritanian Desert in North Africa during the Dakar Rally, probably the toughest enduro race of all.*

TECHNICAL DATA

These are the main types of off-road competition:

- *Motocross*
- *Supercross*
- *Supermotard*
- *Enduro*
- *Desert racing (a type of enduro)*

OFF-ROAD FLYERS

Motocross bikes have an amazing combination of light weight and big power. Sneak a ride on a competition bike and you'll probably end up lying on the ground wondering what happened. With a bite as bad as their bark, these bikes will spit you off in the blink of an eye.

Open-faced helmet

Goggles

Body armor

Gloves

Knee pads

Protective boots

▷ A fully suited young motocross rider races during a junior dirt track race in Sweden.

SUSPENSION

The impact of the massive jumps and big bumps of a motocross course could easily break a rider's arms. This is why MX bikes are fitted with long-travel suspension to soak up the force of the impact. The suspension usually has about 12 inches (30 cm) of **travel**.

TECHNICAL DATA

GOAT (which stands for "Greatest Of All Time") is the nickname of Ricky Carmichael, the best MX and SX racer ever. By 2007, when he retired at age 27, Ricky had won over 100 top-level races.

ENGINE

MX and SX bikes are the same. They usually have four-stroke engines, which are quieter than the old two-strokes—but still noisy and smoky! The engines are so powerful that gripping the handlebars can feel a bit like riding a bucking bronco or rodeo bull.

BRAKES AND TIRES

Whether it's for breathtaking acceleration or eye-popping grip, an MX bike's knobbly tires are perfect—even in the muddiest conditions. There are brakes on both wheels, and they stop the lightweight bikes almost instantly, with the front brakes doing most of the work.

A DAY AT THE (OFF-ROAD) RACES

Motocross and supercross are unusual motorsports because there's no starting grid. Instead, everyone starts in a line together. This makes for very exciting starts—and quite a lot of crashes!

THE HOLE SHOT

The racers are held back at the start line by a barrier. When the barrier flops down toward them, the race is on! Everyone wants to get to the first corner—the hole shot—ahead of the pack.

◁ The start of a motocross race is guaranteed to make your heart beat faster.

MOTOS

Each race is called a **moto**. How long the moto lasts is decided either by distance (for example, 5 laps) or time plus distance (for example, 30 minutes plus 2 laps). In a big contest, the top riders from each moto go through to the next round, and so on until there is a winner.

▷ *Mud covers a rider during a moto. The riders have to be extremely fit. A recent investigation found that they put more strain on their bodies than almost any other athletes.*

SPECIALTY RACES

There are quite a few specialty races in a motocross season. One of the most famous is at Le Touquet in France. Hundreds of riders spend three hours trying to steer their bikes through the town's slippy, slidy, engine-clogging sand dunes.

TECHNICAL DATA

Loop the loop! In 2002, Caleb Wyatt became the first motocross rider to land a backflip. In 2007, Travis Pastrana went one better with a double backflip.

RACING AROUND THE WORLD

Motorcycle races take place on every continent except Antarctica—and even there, there is the possibility of racing on ice. But where are the best race circuits?

THE NÜRBURGRING

On race days, Germany's Nürburgring is closed to ordinary vehicles. But the track is open to the public when there's no racing going on. Coming around a corner to find a tractor pacing along in front of you makes riding there very challenging!

▽ *A 250cc rider negotiates a **chicane** at the Nürburgring in Germany during qualifying for a race.*

SEVLIEVO, BULGARIA

The motocross track at Sevlievo, Bulgaria, mixes long uphill sections with scary downhills and a wide track that's perfect for overtaking. The track is so popular that it was voted the world's best off-road circuit in 2006 and 2007.

▽ Riders take the first corner in an MX world championship race in Sevlievo, Bulgaria.

THE DAKAR ROUTE

This was probably the hardest motorcycle race in the world. The route of this rally went from southern Europe to Dakar in North Africa, crossing the Sahara Desert. In 2008, the race was cancelled for fear of terrorist attacks, and the 2009 race shifted to South America.

TECHNICAL DATA

In 2009, the Dakar Rally started almost 4,350 miles (7,000 km) from Dakar—in Buenos Aires, Argentina. It then did a 3,700 mile (6,000 km) loop around South America before finishing back at Buenos Aires.

GLOSSARY

bhp
Short for brake horsepower, a way of measuring how powerful an engine is. The more bhp an engine has, the more powerful it is.

bonus
When riders win, they may be paid a bonus by their team. In top level racing, this bonus is shared among the support team.

cc
Short for cubic centimeters, a measure of the size of an engine.

chaotic
Disorganized and messy, or not governed by any clear rules.

chicane
A series of corners on a racetrack, often in the form of an "S" shape.

cinder
In motor racing, cinders are small pieces of rock that are used as the surface of a race track during dirt-track races.

constructors' championship
Competition between motor racing teams, based on which team scores the most points over the whole of a racing season.

endo
Motorcycle trick where the rider stops so hard that the back wheel lifts up in the air, and balances on the front wheel.

long-travel suspension
Describes suspension that has a lot of shock-absorbing ability.

moto
Motocross or supercross race.

pit boss
Person who manages a rider's support team of engineers and mechanics.

podium
Place where the top three finishers are awarded their prizes.

pole position
Place at the front of the starting grid.

production motorcycles
Motorcycles that are sold in large quantities.

satellite teams
Racing teams that are linked to a factory team. Satellite teams usually get improved parts for their motorcycles after the factory riders have had a chance to use them.

season
Period from the start to the finish of a racing championship.

starting grid
Lineup of riders at the start of a race. Usually the fastest rider is at the front.

travel
Amount of shock absorption in a motorcycle's suspension.

STAR RIDERS

RICKY CARMICHAEL
MX AND SX

Born: November 27, 1979
Nationality: American

The most successful MX rider ever. He recorded perfect seasons in 2002 and 2004, winning every race he entered.

JUTTA KLEINSCHMIDT
DESERT RACING

Born: August 29, 1962
Nationality: German

Kleinschmidt is most famous for her racing in the Dakar Rally. She first raced Dakar on bikes, then in 2001 she won in a car.

STÉPHANE PETERHANSEL
DESERT RACING

Born: August 6, 1965
Nationality: French

The best desert racer ever. He has won the Dakar Rally nine times—six times on a motorcycle, three in a car.

VALENTINO ROSSI
MotoGP

Born: February 16, 1979
Nationality: Italian

By 2008, "The Doctor" (Rossi's nickname) had won eight world championships, six of them in the top class of racing.

JAMES "BUBBA" STEWART
MX AND SX

Born: December 21, 1985
Nationality: American

After a brilliant junior career, Stewart won the American Motorcycle Association supercross title in 2007.

CASEY STONER
MotoGP

Born: October 16, 1985
Nationality: Australian

Stoner first raced a motorcycle at the age of four and became the second-youngest top-class world champion ever in 2007.

WEB SITES

www.motocrossactionmag.com/ME2/Default.asp
This web site features product reviews and bike tests for bikes in motocross. It also showcases a variety of photos and race reviews.

www.racerxonline.com/
Breaking news in motocross and supercross events, along with blogs, video clips, and pictures.

www.supercross.com
Detailed profiles of riders, race results, and upcoming events are all included in this web site. The web site also includes a supercross community, along with pictures and videos of the most recent races.

www.amaproracing.com
The homepage of the American Motorcycle Association—Professional Racing which carries up-to-date results of races. Along with information on different racetracks, it also includes information for motocross, supercross, ATV, and hillclimb.

INDEX